Helen Keller
Courageous Learner and Leader

written by Amanda Doering Tourville   illustrated by Richard Stergulz

Content Consultant:
Jan Seymour-Ford, Research Librarian
Perkins School for the Blind

magic
wagon

JB
Keller
T

visit us at www.abdopublishing.com

Printed in the United States of America, North Mankato, Minnesota.
092012
012013

 THIS BOOK CONTAINS AT LEAST 10% RECYCLED MATERIALS.

Text by Amanda Doering Tourville
Illustrations by Richard Stergulz
Edited by Holly Saari
Series design by Emily Love
Cover and interior production by Craig Hinton

Library of Congress Cataloging-in-Publication Data

Tourville, Amanda Doering, 1980-
  Helen Keller : courageous learner and leader / by Amanda Doering Tourville ; illustrated by Richard
Stergulz.
     p. cm. – (Beginner biographies)
  ISBN 978-1-61641-938-7
1. Deaf children–Means of communication–Juvenile literature. 2. Blind children–Juvenile literature. I. Title.
  HV2392.T68 2013
  362.4'1092–dc23
  [B]
                            2012026515

Table of Contents

Deaf and Blind

Helen Adams Keller was born on June 27, 1880, in Tuscumbia, Alabama. Helen was a normal baby. At six months old, she could say a few words. She took her first steps at one year old. Then, when Helen was about one and a half, she became sick. No one knew what the illness was. But it left Helen blind and deaf.

Helen could see and hear
when she was born.

Helen had to try to find other ways to communicate with her family.

Helen stopped talking. She found other ways to tell people what she wanted. She would pull on their clothes to tell them to come. Or she'd push them away so they would leave her alone.

Helen was smart and curious, but she was also impatient and bossy. She became upset when people could not understand her. She would kick and scream. Sometimes she hurt herself or others.

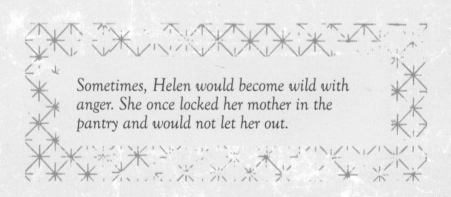

Sometimes, Helen would become wild with anger. She once locked her mother in the pantry and would not let her out.

A New Teacher

When Helen was six years old, her parents took her to a doctor in Baltimore, Maryland. They hoped he could fix her eyes, but he could not.

Even so, the doctor changed Helen's life. He told her parents to contact another doctor, Alexander Graham Bell. Dr. Bell told Helen's parents about a school for the blind in Boston, Massachusetts. Soon, they found a teacher for Helen. The teacher had once attended the school. Her name was Anne Mansfield Sullivan.

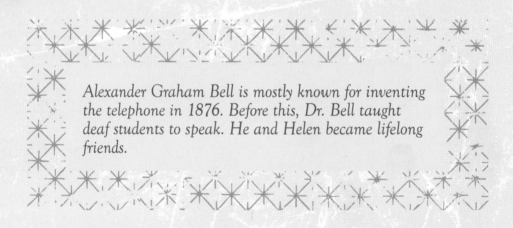

Alexander Graham Bell is mostly known for inventing the telephone in 1876. Before this, Dr. Bell taught deaf students to speak. He and Helen became lifelong friends.

Dr. Bell helped Helen and her
parents find a teacher.

Helen learned the word *water*
by feeling it on her hands.

Helen was almost seven years old when Anne came to her home in Alabama. The teacher and student went straight to work. Anne had brought Helen a doll. With her finger, Anne traced d-o-l-l into Helen's palm.

Another time, Anne ran cool water over Helen's hand. Then Anne spelled *water* on her palm. Helen learned that everything had a name. She learned how to show what she was thinking.

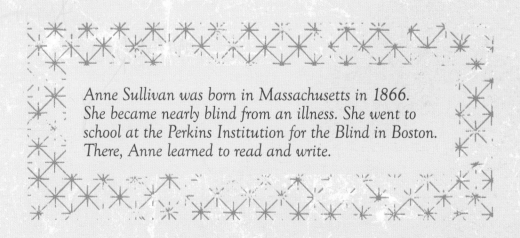

Anne Sullivan was born in Massachusetts in 1866. She became nearly blind from an illness. She went to school at the Perkins Institution for the Blind in Boston. There, Anne learned to read and write.

A Fast Learner

Helen was excited to learn the name of everything she touched. Anne also taught Helen words for things that can't be touched, such as *love* and *think*.

As Helen learned more words, Anne taught her about the world. The two often worked outdoors. Helen loved to be where she could feel and smell nature. Helen and Anne became very close.

Helen and Anne liked to work outdoors.

Helen read by feeling raised
dots on a page.

Anne gave Helen pieces of cardboard with words on them. The letters were raised so Helen could trace them with her fingers. Then Helen used letters to make words herself. By doing this, Helen was learning to read.

Helen matched words with their objects. She learned to put words together to make sentences. Like other children, she began reading simple books. Helen learned to read braille. Instead of seeing the words, Helen felt them on paper.

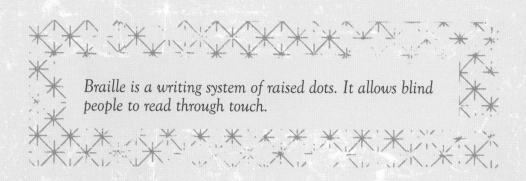

Braille is a writing system of raised dots. It allows blind people to read through touch.

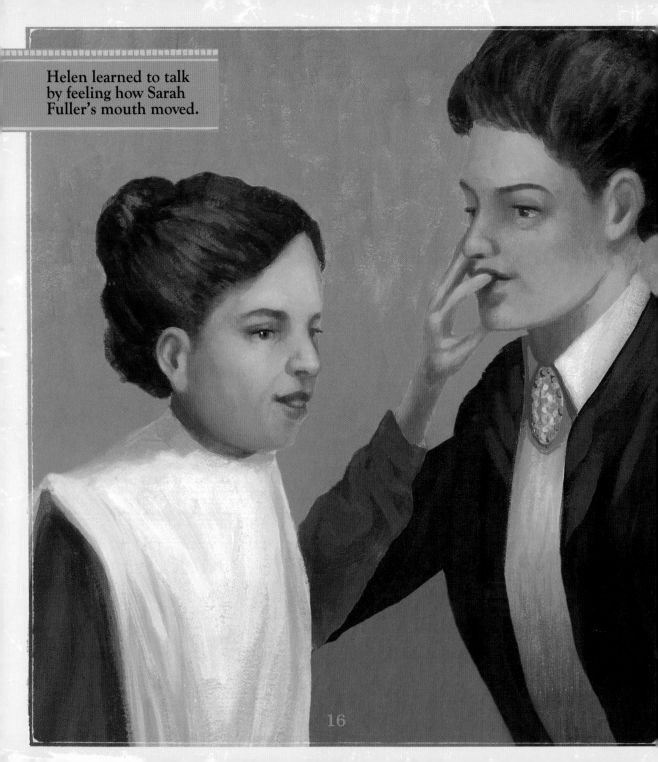

Helen learned to talk by feeling how Sarah Fuller's mouth moved.

Helen wanted to learn to speak, too. When she was ten, Helen begged Anne to take her to see Sarah Fuller, a teacher of the deaf. Sarah agreed to work with Helen. Sarah had Helen touch her face and lips while she talked. Helen would then copy the way Sarah's face moved.

After many hours of practice, Helen began to speak. It took Helen a long time to speak correctly. Anne gently corrected her when she said words the wrong way.

Off to School

When Helen was 16, she went to Cambridge School for Young Ladies in Massachusetts. She studied many subjects. Anne went to classes with Helen. In Helen's hand, Anne wrote what each teacher was saying. Anne used this method to teach Helen what was in her schoolbooks, too.

Helen's time at Cambridge School was very difficult. She left after just one year. But she continued to learn from a tutor.

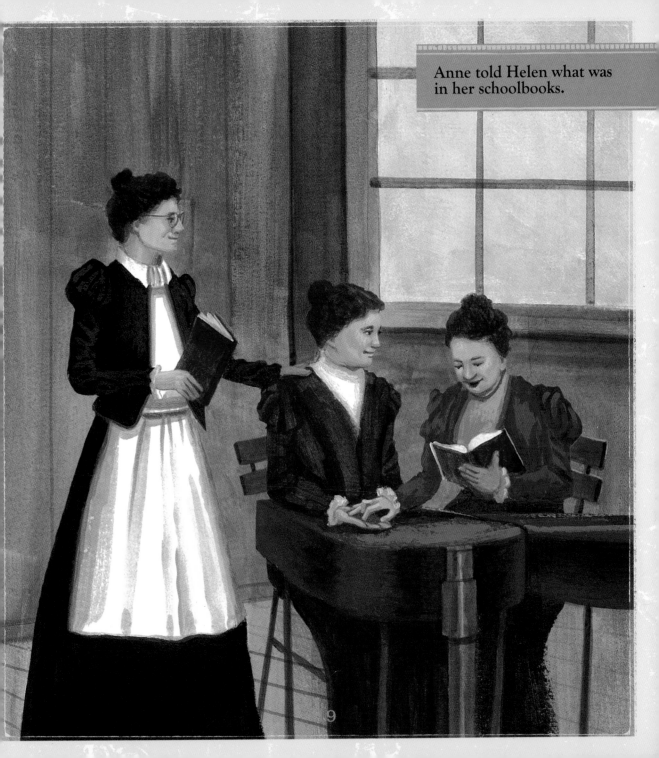

Anne told Helen what was in her schoolbooks.

Even as a young girl, Helen had wanted to go to college. At the age of 20, she entered Radcliffe College in Cambridge, Massachusetts. Helen studied languages and history. She was very busy. Helen used a special typewriter to write her papers.

Helen started writing a book. *The Story of My Life* came out in 1902. Helen wrote about how she had learned to speak and read. Her book sold poorly at first but has now become famous.

Helen used a special typewriter to do her schoolwork and to write a book.

In June 1904, Helen graduated from college. She was the first deaf and blind person to have ever done so. She became famous for her amazing success.

Helen kept writing. She wrote articles for newspapers and magazines. She wrote about her life. She also wrote about politics and equal rights for women. Helen wrote more books, too.

Helen graduated from Radcliffe College.

Helen met President Calvin Coolidge during her travels.

Helping the Blind

Helen wanted to help blind people. She joined groups, such as the American Federation for the Blind. She helped raise money for the group. In 1914, Helen and Anne began traveling around the country and the world. They gave talks about Helen's life. Helen inspired people with her story.

Then in 1936, Anne died. She was 70 years old. Helen was heartbroken. Anne had been her teacher and friend for nearly 50 years. The two women had rarely been apart.

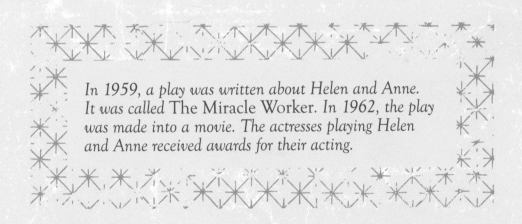

In 1959, a play was written about Helen and Anne. It was called The Miracle Worker. In 1962, the play was made into a movie. The actresses playing Helen and Anne received awards for their acting.

Helen's secretary, Polly Thomson, took over many of Anne's duties. Helen and Polly continued to travel around the world.

When World War II began, Helen went to Europe. She visited wounded soldiers in hospitals. Some of them became blind in the war. Helen brought them hope. She showed them they could still do many things.

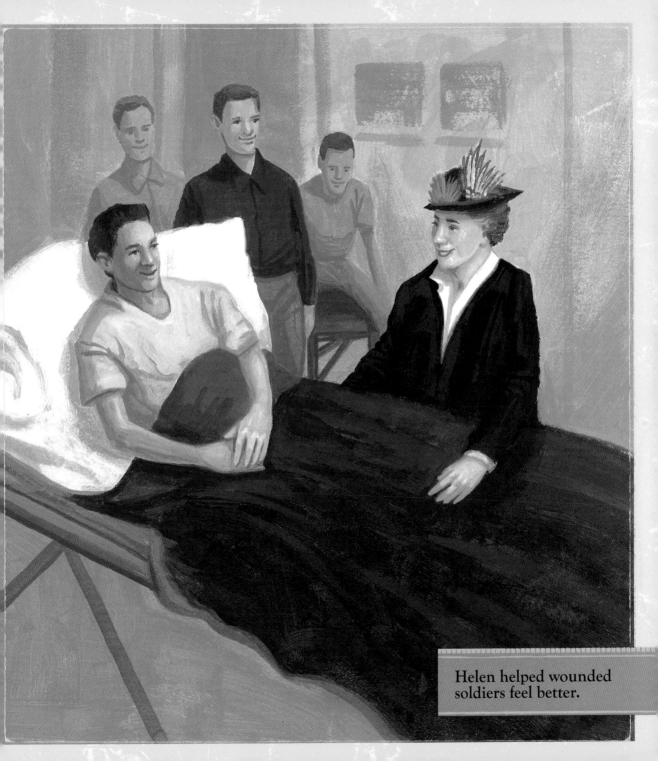

Helen helped wounded soldiers feel better.

President Lyndon Johnson gave the
Presidential Medal of Freedom to Helen.

28

An Inspiring Life

In 1961, Helen stopped traveling and giving speeches. In 1964, President Lyndon Johnson awarded Helen the Presidential Medal of Freedom. It was a great honor.

Helen died at her home in Connecticut on June 1, 1968. She was 87 years old. Her life continues to inspire people around the world.

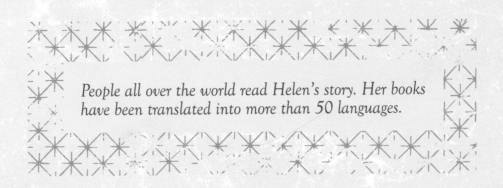

People all over the world read Helen's story. Her books have been translated into more than 50 languages.

FUN FACTS

✦ Soon after Anne Sullivan arrived at the Kellers' house, Helen locked Anne in her room. She would not let Anne out. Helen's father had to rescue Anne by climbing a ladder to her window.

✦ Helen Keller once said that she had met every president from Grover Cleveland (1888–1889 and 1893–1897) to John F. Kennedy (1961–1963).

✦ Helen visited more than 35 countries on five continents.

TIMELINE

1880 Helen Adams Keller was born on June 27, in Tuscumbia, Alabama.

1882 Helen became ill in February and lost her hearing and sight.

1887 Anne Sullivan began teaching Helen.

1890 Helen began to learn to speak with Sarah Fuller.

1896 Helen attended the Cambridge School for Young Ladies for one year.

1902 Helen's first book, *The Story of My Life*, was published.

1904 Helen graduated from Radcliffe College.

1914 Helen and Anne began traveling in the United States and abroad.

1936 Anne Sullivan died.

1964 President Lyndon Johnson honored Helen with the Presidential Medal of Freedom.

1968 Helen died on June 1 in Connecticut.

GLOSSARY

braille—a system of writing for the blind that uses raised dots.

graduate—to finish high school, college, or another course of study.

inspire—to encourage or influence others.

politics—the art or science of governing a city, a state, or a country.

rights—things people can have or do according to the law.

secretary—a person who handles the correspondence and daily work for an office or person.

translate—to transfer from one language into another so it can be understood.

tutor—someone who teaches a student privately.

LEARN MORE

At the Library

DeVillier, Christy. *Helen Keller*. Edina, MN: Abdo, 2004.

Fetty, Margaret. *Helen Keller: Break Down the Walls!* New York: Bearport, 2007.

Koestler-Grack, Rachel A. *The Story of Helen Keller*. Philadelphia, PA: Chelsea Clubhouse, 2004.

On the Web

To learn more about Helen Keller, visit ABDO Group online at **www.abdopublishing.com**. Web sites about Keller are featured on our Book Links page. These links are routinely monitored and updated to provide the most current information available.

INDEX